Migration to Australia

19th Century

Pearson Australia
(a division of Pearson Australia Group Pty Ltd)
707 Collins Street, Melbourne, Victoria 3008
PO Box 23360, Melbourne, Victoria 8012
www.pearson.com.au

First published 2012 by Pearson Australia
2018 2017 2016
10 9 8 7 6 5 4 3

Author: Liz Flaherty
Publisher: Sarah Russell
Project Editor: Rachel Davis
Editor: Angela Tannous
Designers: Anne Donald, Justin Lim
Copyright & Pictures Editor: Alice McBroom
Cover designer: Glen McClay
Printed in Australia by the SOS Print + Media Group

National Library of Australia Cataloguing-in-Publication entry
Author: Flaherty, Liz, 1963-
Title: 19th century / Liz Flaherty.
ISBN: 9781442559912 (pbk.)
Series: Migration.
Notes: Includes index.
Target Audience: For primary school age.
Subjects: History, Modern--19th century--Textbooks.
Australia--History--19th century--Textbooks.
Dewey Number: 994.02

Pearson Australia Group Pty Ltd ABN 40 004 245 943

Acknowledgements
We would like to thank the following for permission to reproduce copyright material.
The following abbreviations are used in this list: t = top, b = bottom, l = left, r = right, c = centre.

Alamy: p. 21.
Corbis: Bettmann, p. 11.
Dreamstime: p. 17tb.
National Library of Australia: p. 5t (nla.pic-an6016104); p. 13t (nla.pic-an9928451); p. 15t (nla.pic-an7746558); p. 15b (nla.pic-an7342551); p. 23b (nla.pic-an24615958); p. 29t (nla.pic-an11030057-405).
Pearson Australia: Alice McBroom, p. 19t.
Shutterstock: cover.
State Library of NSW: p. 5b (GPO 2-06724); p. 7t (a928309); p. 7b (824187); p. 9 (a2331001); p. 13b (a140031).
State Library of Victoria: pp. 18–19 (mp012666); p. 23t (H89.266/19); p. 25 (mp007524); p. 27 (mp007062); p. 29b (H21862).

Every effort has been made to trace and acknowledge copyright. However, if any infringement has occurred, the publishers tender their apologies and invite the copyright holders to contact them.

Some of the images used in *Migration to Australia: 19th Century* might have associations with deceased Indigenous Australians. Please be aware that these images might cause sadness or distress in Aboriginal or Torres Strait Islander communities.

Contents

Words that are printed in bold are explained in the Glossary on page 31.

Introduction

Australia is a nation that has been built on migration. Migration is the movement of people from one nation, place or location to another. Since 1788, people from many nations and cultures have come to Australia to make this land their home. But, many thousands of years before 1788, another wave of people came to Australia. These people are Australia's first inhabitants—the Aboriginal and Torres Strait Islander peoples.

Why People Migrate

People migrate for different reasons. Some people are forced to migrate because a natural disaster has destroyed their home and their community. When people in this situation migrate, they are doing so for environmental reasons. Some people are forced to leave their country because of war or because they are **persecuted** for their political or religious beliefs. These people are moving for political or religious reasons.

Many people move to another country for a better life or to be near family members who have moved. These people are moving for social reasons. Finally, other people move to a different country because they or their employer believes there are better career opportunities for them in that country. These people are moving for economic reasons.

Migration

Migration is either permanent or temporary—that is, people leave their home forever or for only a certain period of time. When a person leaves a country, he or she is said to be *emigrating*. When a person arrives in a country, he or she is said to be *immigrating*.

About This Book

This book explores migration to Australia during the 19th century. At the start of the century, convicts made up the majority of the population of New South Wales. But **free settlers** were migrating from Britain in increasing numbers. Agriculture was an important and growing industry in Australia, and the British government's offer of free convict labour attracted many British migrants.

The population grew steadily, and by the end of the 1860s, there were six separate Australian colonies: New South Wales, Tasmania, Queensland, Victoria, South Australia and Western Australia. Each colony had its own government, but they were still part of the British Empire. Many British immigrants thought of themselves as British people living in another country. As the 19th century progressed, people from different countries began migrating to Australia. Australia began to develop its own culture, and there was a gradual push towards independence from Britain, which led to Federation in 1901.

A view of Sydney painted in 1810 shows the growing infrastructure across the land.

In 1790, Elizabeth Macarthur arrived in Sydney Cove with her husband Captain John Macarthur.

Population of New South Wales

By 1800, only 12 years after European settlement in 1788, one in six European people was born in the colony. A **census** was taken in 1805 that gave the governor of New South Wales and the British government important information about how many people lived in the colony.

The 1805 Census

The 1805 census showed that there were approximately 7000 people living in the colony of New South Wales. There were 4000 men, 1300 women and 1700 children, of whom 2000 were convicts and 600 were officials. The census also showed that there were approximately 20 000 sheep and Captain John Macarthur owned one quarter of them.

The population of New South Wales grew steadily, but there was an increasing lack of free labour. The colony needed more workers to make the land **prosper**. By 1806, there were 610 **free settlers**. So far, the colony was huddled along the coast, but people were beginning to wonder what lay inland and further along the coastal regions.

Convicts

Many convicts transported to New South Wales before 1800 had been granted a **ticket of leave**, which meant they could work for themselves and own property. Governor Arthur Phillip had introduced the ticket of leave. For the many convicts who received one, this was a wonderful opportunity. It offered a better life than would have been possible in England. There, life was still difficult for poor people. Some could hardly afford to feed or clothe themselves or their families, and there was no government assistance. Even though the early years in the colony had been challenging, with food shortages and **rations**, life was better in the colony than back home.

New Governor

Philip Gidley King arrived with the First Fleet in 1788. After his term as Lieutenant Governor of Norfolk Island, King was appointed governor of New South Wales in 1800. Governor King had two children with a convict named Ann Inett whom he had met on Norfolk Island.

The colony prospered under King's leadership. Governor King treated the Aboriginal peoples with some compassion. But even though King thought of them as the true owners of the land, he still gave away large **land grants** to new settlers. King tried to protect the Aboriginals from diseases by introducing vaccinations, but it was too late for most of them. Many Aboriginal peoples were already sick with or had died from the diseases.

New South Wales Corps

A large number of the officers and men, who made up the New South Wales Corps under Captain John Macarthur, chose to settle in the colony when they were **discharged**. They were given land grants and the use of convicts to work their land.

The Aboriginal peoples were pushed further away from their land and were not included in the census.

Wine Industry

In 1800, the British government sent two French prisoners to the colony of New South Wales for three years to establish a wine industry and teach others how to produce wine. The men were paid for their work. They planted 12 000 vines at Parramatta. The new environment was challenging and they only produced 40 gallons of wine by 1804. In 1814, Governor Lachlan Macquarie instructed Doctor William Redfern to investigate convict deaths on transport ships. Doctor Redfern recommended a pint of wine each day to prevent malnutrition. This gave the colony a good reason to grow grapes, and the wine industry gradually took off.

Governor Philip Gidley King contributed greatly to the early years of the colony.

New Settlements and Emancipists

Governor King was a naval officer and encouraged exploration by sea. After Matthew Flinders and George Bass discovered in 1799 that Van Diemen's Land (Tasmania) was separated from the mainland by Bass Strait, King set his sights on occupying the island. King and the British government were worried that the French would settle Van Diemen's Land before they did. King was also keen to relocate some of Sydney's convicts to somewhere else.

Van Diemen's Land

A settlement in Van Diemen's Land was founded in September 1803. At first, peaceful relations were established with the Aboriginal peoples. By 1810, there were approximately 12000 people living on the island and a few small schools had been established. The new colony received its first convicts in 1812. After Norfolk Island was abandoned in 1814, its inhabitants were transferred to Van Diemen's Land.

Governor Bligh

William Bligh arrived in New South Wales in August 1806 to replace Governor King. As governor, Bligh tried to reform the colony by stopping the **lucrative** rum trade that was controlled by the officers of the New South Wales Corps. Lieutenant George Johnston, with the help of John Macarthur and other powerful people in the colony, overthrew Governor Bligh because they did not like his reforms. Bligh was a threat to the power the corps held in the colony.

Governor Macquarie

Lachlan Macquarie, a Scottish soldier, became governor of New South Wales in January 1810. Macquarie brought his own regiment of 700 soldiers to replace the **corrupt** New South Wales Corps.

Macquarie provided stability for the colonies. He built roads, schools, barracks, a hospital and other permanent public buildings. Macquarie established new townships around Sydney and encouraged exploration of the land. The country was filling up with settlers between the coast and the Blue Mountains.

Macquarie thought that emancipated convicts deserved the same rights as other **free settlers**. Not everyone agreed with this view, and there was social division between ex-convicts and the free settlers. Many free settlers did not want to mix or associate with newly freed convicts.

Grateful Emancipists

According to Governor Macquarie, the best settlers were the **emancipists** because they appreciated their opportunities. They worked hard and **cultivated** the land they were given. Macquarie told the British government that the free settlers were ungrateful and expected handouts from the government. The free settlers seemed to think the government owed them favours just because they had migrated to Australia.

Governor Lachlan Macquarie chose Matthew Flinders' suggestion of "Australia" as the continent's name. Macquarie became known as "The Father of Australia".

Back in Britain

During the late 18th and early 19th centuries, there were great changes taking place in Britain. Many people depended on agriculture or **manual labour** to earn a living, but new technologies were changing the way things had been done for centuries. Jobs and tasks that were once done by hand could now be done by machines. The Industrial Revolution was underway.

From Handmade to Machine-Made

The textile industry was one of the first industries to move from handmade goods to machine-made. Because there was a large demand for cloth, merchants had to compete with others for supplies to make the cloth, which added to the cost. The solution to the added cost was machinery. With the invention of the steam engine, textile goods could be made faster and cheaper than if they were made by people. So, machinery replaced many people in the workforce. As only wealthy people could afford an education, textile workers who lost their jobs found it very difficult to find other employment.

Factories sprang up in cities, and many people moved from country areas to the cities in the hope of finding work. But unemployment across Britain was extremely high. Cities in England were already crowded, so living conditions became even worse. Many poor families crowded together in one bedroom just to have a roof over their heads. There was no running water, no heating and no bathroom. Human waste was thrown into the streets and mixed with dirt, rubbish and rats. Diseases such as **cholera** and **dysentery** were common.

For those with jobs, the working conditions were often terrible. Employers wanted to make a lot of money and had little or no concern for the wellbeing of their employees. Child labour was common. Children were even sent to work in factories and coal mines. The little money they earned helped to keep their families alive.

The Great Migration

Because so many people were out of work, the rate of crime increased. People were desperate to escape and find a better life for themselves and their families. This period of time became known as the Great Migration. People emigrated from all over Britain, especially from Ireland, to either Australia or the United States of America. Those who could never afford to own property in their homeland were offered free transport, free land and free convict labour. The offer of migration was too good to pass up. Australia was the land of new opportunities.

Migration was a brave move in the early 19th century. Most people knew no one else in Australia, and the journey to the other side of the world was long and dangerous. But, for some people, anything seemed better than living in absolute poverty back in Britain.

Using child labour in coal mines helped

poor families to survive.

The Colonies

When Governor Lachlan Macquarie resigned as governor of New South Wales in 1822, there were approximately 25 000 people in the colony. Two-thirds of them were either convicts or **emancipists**. Australians born from European settlers were very proud of the colonies and the fact that they were Australian. By the mid-1820s, Australia was developing into a country that was seen as suitable for middle-class British settlers, not just people from the lower classes escaping poverty and unemployment. There were numerous opportunities to **prosper**.

Wakefield's Migration Plan

Edward Wakefield was a criminal who spent three years in Newgate Prison in England for abducting a 15-year-old girl. Although Wakefield had never been to Australia, he came up with an idea for a new way to develop Australia while he was in prison in 1829.

Wakefield thought the best way to populate the new colonies was with good British stock, not the lower classes or more convicts. His idea to entice the middle-class English to Australia was to charge people for the land and offer them free labour. He thought free land would only encourage poor people, which wouldn't be good for the colonies. If the price for land was set high enough, the poor would not be able to afford to migrate, while the middle classes could.

In 1831, Wakefield's idea became popular, although it never really worked. **Squatters** had already taken up vast amounts of land in New South Wales and would never consider paying for land they were already on, and the best land was already gone in Van Diemen's Land. South Australia seemed the perfect place for Wakefield's plan, and it led to immigration being seen as an acceptable thing to do.

Land Sales

By 1831, the British government was offering free immigration, but it had discontinued free **land grants**. In 1831, land in New South Wales sold for five **shillings** an acre. Money from the land sales was used to help many poor English and Irish people to migrate to Australia. Between 1832 and 1836, the sum of 125 000 **pounds** was raised in the sale of land. This was used to send 40 000 migrants and 35 000 convicts to Australia by the end of the 1830s. For the first time, the **immigrants** in the colony outnumbered the native-born Australians.

Queensland

Queensland was part of New South Wales in the early days of settlement. Brisbane was established in 1825 as a penal colony for convicts who were difficult to control. The penal settlement was officially closed in 1839. Land was prepared for sale for permanent settlement.

The 1828 Census

In 1828, Aboriginal peoples were still not considered citizens of Australia and so were not included in the **census**. There were around 36 598 European people spread across the country. One-third of them lived in Sydney and there were three times as many men as women.

Edward Wakefield encouraged migration to the new colonies.

A colonial homestead. Life was becoming more comfortable for some in the colonies.

Migration to the West and South

Western Australia and South Australia were settled differently from the other colonies. Neither of them was a penal colony, although Western Australia did receive some convicts. Western Australia was in an excellent position to provide a trade link to China, India and islands to the north. It also made a convenient stopping point between Britain and the eastern colonies.

Western Australia

Western Australia offered a good climate, abundant water and reasonable soil for crops. Settling the west would also prevent the French from taking possession of the western part of Australia, something the British government had always worried about. On 2 May 1829, Captain Charles Fremantle took possession of the western third of the country on behalf of the British government. The British government handed out 250 000 acres of land to **free settlers**. There was no offer of free convict labour, which was given to settlers on the east coast.

More than 4000 people had settled in Western Australia by 1830. But only 1500 settlers remained two years later, as people struggled to work the land without free convict labour. By 1832, the government charged five **shillings** per acre. The English lost interest in migrating to Western Australia now that they had to pay for the land.

South Australia

South Australia was proclaimed a colony in 1836 by Governor John Hindmarsh. In 1841, South Australia had 12 000 **assisted migrants**. Assisted migrants received free transport to Australia. No convicts were sent to the colony, which gave it a good reputation compared to the penal colonies.

Many settlers from Germany arrived in South Australia from 1836. They settled in places such as Klemzig, Hahndorf, Kangaroo Island and the Barossa Valley. In 1838, many **Lutheran** Germans immigrated because of **religious persecution**. They wanted the freedom to practise their religion in peace. After the King of **Prussia** died in 1840, Germans migrated to Australia for economic, not religious, reasons. Word had spread in Germany of the fine crops such as wheat, barley and oats that were being grown.

Governor Hindmarsh was impressed with the German migrants. Information about the colony was distributed in Germany in the hope of encouraging more migrants to come to South Australia. Many of the early German **immigrants** were very poor, and Australia seemed to offer good opportunities.

German Migrants

The German immigrants in South Australia were hardworking people and contributed greatly to the success of South Australia as a colony. They brought many skills and knowledge with them and created industries such as silversmithing, winemaking and weaving. German people were proud of their culture and maintained their customs and language as much as they could. German schools were set up wherever they went.

Western Australia was settled much later than the eastern part of Australia.

Around five per cent of all German migrants came to escape religious persecution, and many settled in parts of South Australia.

Irish Potato Famine

Ireland was part of Britain in the 19th century. Many Irish people lived in great poverty and struggled to feed and clothe their families. Potatoes were an important source of food and many people depended on them for their survival. Boiled potatoes were usually eaten three times a day. When, in the 1840s, a potato famine struck the Irish, many started migrating to Australia.

Disaster Strikes

In the mid-1840s, a disastrous disease struck potato crops over the whole of Ireland. An airborne fungus rotted the plants and the potatoes. The British government official in charge of providing relief for the Irish thought it was best for them to solve their own problems. He thought food handouts would only make them more dependent on the government.

Famine Sets In

While the Irish began to starve, oats and grain that were grown on Irish soil were sent by the shipload to England. Riots spread across Ireland. England sent in troops to control the masses. People were desperate and ate anything they could find—including seaweed, nettles, blackberries, weeds and even grass. People died in their homes and by the roadside. No one had the energy to bury people properly, so many were buried without a coffin just below the surface of the soil.

The famine lasted five years. The English had little or no compassion for the Irish, and many **landlords** even threw **tenants** off their properties. Over one million Irish died during the famine. Around 23 000 Irish people migrated to Australia for their own survival and in search of a better life.

Irish Orphan Girls

More than 4000 female Irish orphans were shipped to Australia under a plan known as "Earl Grey's Famine Orphan Scheme". The girls came from workhouses situated all over Ireland. Many of them had no parents or their parents had placed them in the workhouses because they couldn't afford to feed them. The girls were aged between 14 and 20. They were offered free passage to Australia to become **domestic servants**.

Life was so bad in Ireland that the prospect of a new life in Australia appealed to many of the girls. The British government wanted girls to migrate to Australia to help balance the ratio of men to women in the colony. Around 2000 girls lived at Hyde Park Barracks in Sydney until they found work.

Hyde Park Barracks

Hyde Park Barracks was built in 1819 to house convict men and women. The barracks teemed with thousands of rats. In the 1980s, builders found over 10 000 items hidden under the floorboards. The items included bonnets, aprons, stockings, shirts, food, newspapers and scraps of bedding, which the rats had used to build nests.

These memorial sculptures in Dublin (Ireland) show the hardship that was suffered during the Irish Potato Famine.

Hyde Park Barracks is now a museum.

Highland Clearances

In the late 18th century, an agricultural revolution swept through Scotland. Sheep farming was profitable, and **landlords** wanted to clear larger areas of land to lease to sheep farmers. The sheep farmers paid higher amounts of rent than the poor Scottish highlanders could afford to pay. The population in Scotland grew rapidly between 1800 and 1830, which put increased pressure on the land. Over 500 000 people left the Scottish Highlands, hoping for a better life in places such as the Australian colonies. The massive migration became known as the Highland Clearances.

Scottish Immigrants

In the 1830s, many Scottish people who lived in **clans** in the highlands of Scotland were forced off the land by their landlords to make way for sheep farmers. Many Scottish people were treated brutally and forced out of their houses. Their possessions and little **croft** houses were sometimes burnt in front of them or even with people still inside. Old people, young children and families were thrown out with no regard for their wellbeing.

Some Highlanders moved to coastal areas or cities to try and make a new life. Many of them didn't speak English and couldn't communicate easily with other people. Other highlanders immigrated to Canada and Australia. Over half a million people left the Scottish Highlands hoping for a better life somewhere else. Many Scottish people were assisted with their migration to Australia by the Highland and Island Emigration Society. The society was set up to help Scottish people who were **destitute**.

Traditional clan life was disrupted forever, although many Scottish people tried to keep their culture alive in the colonies through their stories, music and Gaelic language. The first **immigrants** to travel directly to Port Phillip Bay in Victoria arrived in 1839. Most of them were Scottish.

A Scottish Ancestor

Tori Sommer is a sixth-generation Australian. Her ancestor William Robertson immigrated to Australia from Scotland. William and his brother, John, sailed to Van Diemen's Land on the *Regalia* in 1822. There are no records to indicate why William immigrated to Australia, but he made the most of the opportunities available when he arrived.

William became a merchant in Hobart before moving to Victoria, where he established a farm. He also became a member of the Port Phillip Association, which aimed to open up land in southern Australia to settlers. William explored the land near Corio Bay with Joseph Gellibrand. They were guided by William Buckley, who had once lived with the local Aboriginal people.

Tori is interested in her ancestor's story.

Settlements usually hugged rivers or coastlines.

Parkhurst Boys

In the 10 years from 1842 to 1852, 4088 boys were **exiled** to Australia and New Zealand. They came from Parkhurst Prison on the Isle of Wight, England. Parkhurst was a prison for boys between 12 and 18 years of age. The prison aimed to rehabilitate boys and train them in trades such as carpentry, stonework and ironwork that would be useful to society. The Parkhurst boys were not classed as convicts, even though they were transported to Australia in the same way as convicts. The boys were called exiles.

Exiles

Because the boys were called exiles, they were considered to be free in Australia. But they weren't allowed back to Britain until the term of their prison sentence was over. The boys were supposed to be apprenticed to new settlers of the colonies. Many colonists in New South Wales were becoming unhappy about the number of convicts being sent to the colony. They didn't want New South Wales to be viewed as only a penal colony and no longer wanted anything to do with convicts, whom they saw as degrading society. The Parkhurst boys were considered a new solution to the shortage of labour. Colonies that no longer wanted to accept convicts were happy to receive trained labourers. One hundred and thirty-three boys considered unsuitable as apprentices were transported as convicts.

Robert Archman

Robert was only 10 years old when he was charged with stealing rope in Edinburgh, Scotland. Five days later, Robert was charged with stealing a cotton shirt. He pleaded guilty and was sentenced to 20 days in the Edinburgh Prison. Robert continued to steal on his release from prison and was charged with more offences over the next two years. His prison sentences increased to 60 days. In 1844, Robert and a friend were charged with housebreaking and theft. Robert was sentenced on 19 March 1845 to seven years' transportation beyond the seas. Robert was detained at the Edinburgh Prison until his transportation.

Robert was transferred to Parkhurst Prison on the Isle of Wight when he was 13 years old. He then sailed from England as an exile and arrived in Williamstown, Victoria, on board the *Marion* in January 1848. He had a conditional pardon, which meant he could go where he wanted in Australia, but he wasn't allowed to return to Britain until his sentence expired.

Robert lived the rest of his life in Australia. He worked as a farmer or labourer. He married Janet McSwain and had 11 children. Robert and Janet have hundreds of **descendants** living in Australia today.

England. The Parkhurst boys were transported to Western Australia, Tasmania, Victoria, Norfolk Island and New Zealand.

Gold

The discovery of gold brought almost half a million migrants to Victoria during the 1850s. Most of the **immigrants** came from England, Ireland, Scotland, Wales, the United States of America, China and Germany. In just two years, Victoria's population grew from 77 000 people to 540 000.

Chinese Immigrants

Many people in southern China lived in poverty. The prospect of making a fortune from gold lured them to the Victorian goldfields. Many planned to send money back to their families in China. The Victorian government wasn't keen on Chinese immigrants and in 1855 tried to deter them from coming by taxing them 10 **pounds**. The government wanted to keep Australia made up of mostly British people. But this tax was **abolished** in the 1860s, and the Chinese became the fourth largest immigrant group in Victoria after the English, Irish and Germans.

Why the Chinese Migrated

Small numbers of Chinese people had already migrated to the colony of New South Wales from the early days of settlement. The first Chinese person arrived in Australia in 1803. Ahuto was a carpenter and came as a free man. The colony experienced a shortage of workers in the 1800s and landowners recruited Chinese workers because they worked hard for little pay.

When gold was discovered, migration from China to the colonies rose sharply. The Chinese came to search for gold or to set up businesses on the goldfields. Most immigrants were contract labourers, which meant they worked on the goldfields in exchange for their passage to Australia. In 1861, the Chinese made up 3.3 per cent of the population. There were 38 337 men and only 11 women.

Discovery of Gold at Palmer River

In 1873, when gold was discovered at Palmer River in Queensland, many Chinese people flocked to the area. The first Chinese people to arrive came from the goldmines in the southern colonies. By the end of 1874, there were around 4000 Chinese people at Palmer River. They made up 40 per cent of the mining population. As gold continued to be found, more Chinese people arrived from Hong Kong. By 1877, the Chinese people made up 90 per cent of the population at Palmer River.

Much-Needed Skills

Many Chinese migrants had valuable farming skills. From the 1850s, Chinese market gardens supplied most of the food for people living in cities and towns.

Most cities had an area where Chinese people congregated. The areas became known as Chinatown. The Chinese ran successful businesses in furniture making, restaurants, dressmaking and medicine.

Banned from Migrating

In 1888, laws restricting the immigration of Chinese people were introduced. Chinese people were virtually banned from migrating to Australia because of racial discrimination. People also thought the Chinese people would work for less money and take jobs from European Australians.

The Chinese migrants worked very hard in the goldmines.

Many Chinese migrants provided food for the gold-mining population.

Explorers

European settlers had always been keen to explore the interior of the Australian continent. The British government's plan was always to settle the whole continent. By the mid-1800s, expeditions to explore unknown territories were taking place. Explorers usually set out with their supplies loaded on to horses and carts. Some of these expeditions weren't successful and ended in disaster. Horses, donkeys and bullocks needed large amounts of water and food and the horses tired easily in the desert.

Across the Blue Mountains

People had been attempting to cross the Blue Mountains in the west of New South Wales since 1790. Sheer cliffs, rapids, deep gorges and thick scrub made most people turn back. But Gregory Blaxland, with William Lawson and William Charles Wentworth, found the way across.

Blaxland had arrived in New South Wales in 1805. He was keen to find more pasture for his sheep. He made a few trips to the west himself before asking Governor Lachlan Macquarie if he could form an expedition. Blaxland invited William Lawson and William Wentworth to accompany him. Lawson had arrived in the colony in 1799. He was a surveyor before joining the New South Wales Corps. Twenty-one-year-old Wentworth was born in the colony. He had an adventurous spirit and was keen to join the expedition.

The party set out in May 1813 with a local guide, three convict servants, four packhorses and five dogs. The explorers commenced each morning marking out a track, with the guide and one servant, before turning back and clearing a path for the horses to take the next day. After 21 days and 80 kilometres, they reached the top of Mount Blaxland and discovered vast areas of forest and green land to support the stock of the colony.

Search for the Inland Sea

Now that an inland route had been discovered, thoughts turned to opening up the interior of the country for grazing and settlement. Because the country was so large, people thought there must be an inland sea. Surveyors set off in all directions to find it.

George William Evans was the assistant to surveyor general. He was the first European to cross the Great Dividing Range. Evans discovered the Macquarie and the Lachlan rivers. John Oxley, the surveyor general, was impressed with Evan's discoveries. Oxley and Evans set off along the Lachlan River in 1817. They had to turn back when they could not get past marshes. A year later, they followed the Macquarie River and discovered the Castlereagh River, then they went north-east to Port Macquarie.

Charles Sturt

In 1828, Charles Sturt found the source of the Macquarie River and discovered the Bogan and the Darling rivers. Sturt navigated the Murrumbidgee River in a whaleboat and came upon the junction to the Murray River. Sturt was still keen to discover the mythical inland sea so, in 1844, he set out again. He finally reached the Simpson Desert and realised that the inland sea was just a myth.

Blaxland, Lawson and Wentworth successfully crossed the Blue Mountains in 1813.

Thomas Mitchell

Between 1831 and 1836, Thomas Mitchell went on three important expeditions into the interior of Australia. His most important discovery was in 1836. Mitchell followed the course of the Lachlan River to the Murrumbidgee, then crossed country to the Murray River and discovered lush pastureland in western Victoria that he named *Australia Felix* or "Blessed Australia".

Hume and Hovell

Hamilton Hume was born near Parramatta in 1797. He was a keen explorer from the age of 17, and developed a reputation for his excellent bush skills and knowledge of the area south of Parramatta. Governor Macquarie asked Hume to undertake expeditions around Lake Bathurst, Goulburn and Jervis Bay. Hume was rewarded with a land grant where he established a farm.

Hume wanted to attempt an expedition between Lake George and Bass Strait, but he could not come up with the funds. Then he was introduced to William Hovell, who was 11 years older than him. Hovell offered to go with Hume and they shared the cost of the expedition. They set off on 3 October 1824 with four months' worth of supplies.

Hume and Hovell had some differences of opinion about which direction to take, and the exploration party split up at one point. Hovell rejoined Hume after realising that Hume was right and the party struggled on to Corio Bay, near Geelong in Victoria. Their discoveries resulted in the founding of Melbourne. Hume and Hovell bickered for the rest of their lives over who was the right person to take credit for the discovery.

Ludwig Leichhardt

Ludwig Leichhardt was born in **Prussia**. He studied natural sciences in Germany and England before arriving in Sydney in 1842. Leichhardt had poor eyesight and no bush skills at all, but he trekked overland from the Hunter River in New South Wales to Moreton Bay. After this trek, he decided to explore far north Queensland. In 1844, Leichhardt led an expedition to Port Essington. The party crossed vast areas of unexplored territory and at one stage was believed to be lost. People took great interest in what the explorers were doing, so when Leichhardt's party reappeared, the nation was happy.

Leichhardt led another expedition in 1848. His idea was to explore Australia from east to west and down to Perth. In April 1848, he and his party disappeared and no trace of them was ever found. It was believed that they were killed by Aboriginal people.

Burke and Wills

In 1860 and 1861, Robert O'Hara Burke and William John Wills led an expedition of 19 men intending to cross Australia from south to north. At the time, much of Australia's inland remained unexplored by Europeans. The expedition was successful, but seven men lost their lives along the way, including Burke and Wills. Only one man, John King, returned to Melbourne alive.

Explorers had to carry enough equipment for many months away.

Towards a Federated Australia

By the end of the 19th century, there were six separate colonies on the Australian continent. The last of the British troops had left Australia in 1870. The colonies were prosperous, and Sydney and Melbourne had their own universities. There were impressive public buildings in every colony. But as each colony had been self-governing since 1852, there were different systems of trade, transport, defence and even postage. It became obvious that there had to be more cooperation between the colonies.

White Australia Policy

While most people in the colonies were of British origin, there was an increasing number of people from other countries who contributed to Australia's growing identity. But the government and many people of British origin still struggled to accept people from other nations. This was apparent when an economic **depression** in the 1890s brought immigration to a standstill. Cities like Melbourne were in debt, and the prospects for migrants were limited. It was decided at a conference between colonial governments that the restrictions that had been placed on Chinese **immigrants** would include all non-Europeans. Australia's immigration policy became known as the "White Australia policy".

Aboriginal Peoples

Colonial governments also struggled to identify with Australia's first inhabitants. Government rules and regulations for Aboriginal peoples hardened over the 19th century. In 1861, legislation was put in place to confine them to missions and reserves. European Australians tried to make Indigenous peoples dress, behave and work like Europeans. There was no respect for their land or their culture. The control and loss of their rights continued into the late 20th century.

Federation

Towards the end of the 19th century, colonial politicians Henry Parkes, Alfred Deakin and Edmund Barton campaigned to turn the six colonies containing 3.7 million people into one country. Parkes, who was premier of New South Wales five times, became known as the "Father of Federation" for a speech he gave in October 1889. His speech became known as the Tenterfield Address and had an enormous effect on the movement towards federation. Keeping Australia a "white" nation would be one of the goals of the new government.

Between 1898 and 1900, the public voted in favour of federation. Many people were excluded from voting. Indigenous peoples, women, the poor and people of Chinese and Indian **descent** were not allowed to vote. Not many people who were actually eligible to vote chose to do so. The Commonwealth of Australia was proclaimed on 1 January 1901. Most people were in favour of the idea by this stage and turned out to celebrate the new nation. The population of Australia was close to 3.5 million at the end of the century.

Federation was celebrated around the country, including at Centennial Park in Sydney.

Sir Henry Parkes was called the “Father of Federation”.

The New Capital

Politicians could not decide whether Sydney or Melbourne should be the capital city of Australia. So, they decided that a new capital city should be created in New South Wales, which later was called Canberra. Melbourne became the temporary capital after Federation.

Timeline

1788
The First Fleet arrives in Port Jackson.

Late 18th century to early 19th century
An industrial revolution occurs in Britain.

1800
Convicts make up the majority of the migrated population of New South Wales.

1800 to 1806
Philip Gidley King is the governor of New South Wales.

1803
Van Diemen's Land is founded.

1805
A census shows that there are 7000 non-Indigenous peoples in the colony.

1806
There are 610 **free settlers**.

1806
One in six non-indigenous peoples are born in the colony.

1806
Governor Bligh arrives in New South Wales.

1810
12 000 people live in Van Diemen's Land.

1810
Lachlan Macquarie is governor of New South Wales.

1812
The first convicts are sent to Van Diemen's Land.

1814
Convicts from Norfolk Island are sent to Van Diemen's Land.

1822
The population reaches 25 000 nationally.

1822
William Robertson immigrates to Van Diemen's Land.

1828
A census shows that there are 36 598 non-Indigenous peoples in the colony.

1829, May 2
Captain Fremantle takes possession of the western third of Australia.

1830
Over 4000 people live in Western Australia.

1830s
The Highland Clearances occur.

1832
Approximately 1500 people live in Western Australia.

1836
South Australia is proclaimed a colony.

1836
German settlers immigrate to South Australia.

1840s
The Irish Potato Famine occurs.

1841
12 000 **assisted migrants** immigrate to South Australia.

1842 to 1852
4088 boys are exiled to Australia.

1850s
Gold is discovered.

1852
The colonies are self-governing.

1855
A 10-**pound** tax is put on Chinese **immigrants**.

1860
The Burke and Wills expedition takes place.

1861
Chinese people make up 3.3 per cent of the population.

1870
The last of the British troops leave Australia.

1888
Laws restricting Chinese immigration are reintroduced.

1890s
An economic **depression** decreases migration.

Glossary

abolished put an end to; stopped

assisted migrants the government assisted many migrants to Australia by either giving them free transport or paying for part of their transport. The assisted migration schemes were designed to populate the country.

census an official count or survey of the population

cholera an infectious disease that often causes death

clans groups that share the same ancestor, especially in Scotland

corrupt dishonest and accepting bribes

croft a small piece of land used for agriculture in the Scottish highlands. Croft houses were built from stone with the roofs made from wood or straw.

cultivated worked the land to grow crops

depression when the financial situation of a country is in crisis and there is high unemployment

descendants blood relatives in direct line of descent, for example, children, grandchildren and great-grandchildren

descent family origin

destitute extremely poor and unable to feed yourself or your family properly

discharged released from employment

domestic servants people who do work around the home, such as cleaning and cooking

dysentery a disease that causes severe diarrhoea

emancipists convicts who have finished their sentences of seven or 14 years and are free to buy land and work where they want

exiled banished from your own country and not allowed to return

free settlers people who came to the colony as free people and not convicts

immigrants people who come to a country to live

land grants free land given to people from the government

landlords people who own houses, buildings or land that they rent to other people

lucrative profitable; make a lot of money

Lutheran members of a Christian religion based on the teachings of Martin Luther

manual labour physical work using the hands, such as carpentry

persecuted treated cruelly and unfairly because of religious beliefs, race or political ideas

pounds a unit of money used in Britain and used in Australia until 1966

prosper to become rich and successful

Prussia the former kingdom of the German Empire

rations amount of food or clothing allowed for each person

religious persecution being harassed or treated cruelly because of your religious beliefs

shillings a unit of money that was worth approximately 10 cents. It was used in Australia until 1966.

squatters people who occupy land for farming without official government permission

tenants people who rent a house, building or land off a landlord

ticket of leave convicts given a ticket of leave were free from government labour and allowed to work for themselves

Index